FANTASTIC FACTS ABOUT

AUSTRALIA'S INTRIGUING PAST

FRANCES PAYNE

REDBACK publishing

Redback Publishing
Suite 6, 13a Narabang Way,
Belrose NSW 2085
Australia

www.redbackpublishing.com
orders@redbackpublishing.com

Reprinted 2025

978-1-922322-72-2

Author: Frances Payne
Editor: Caroline Thomas
Designer: Redback Publishing

Original illustrations © Redback Publishing 2021
Originated by Redback Publishing

Acknowledgements
Abbreviations: l—left, r—right, b—bottom, t—top, c—centre, m—middle
We would like to thank the following for permission to reproduce photographs: (Images © shutterstock)
p5m Student Action for Aborigines bus ouside the Hotel Bogabilla in February 1965, courtesy of State Library of New South Wales [Public domain], via Wikimedia Commons, p5b Hajime Toyoshima's downed Japanese aircraft, Melville Island, courtesy of Australian War Memorial [Public domain], via Wikimedia Commons, p6m Nova et Accuratissima Terrarum Orbis Tabula, by J.Blaeu, 1664 [Public domain], via Wikimedia Commons, p8b Governor Phillip, portrait by Francis Wheatley [Public domain], via Wikimedia Commons, p9m Chain gang - convicts going to work, by Backhouse, Edward, 1808-1879Backhouse, James, 1794-1869 [Public domain], via Wikmedia Commons, p9bl Battle of Vinegar Hill in the Riot of Castle Hill, courtesy of National Library of Australia [Public domain], p10m Chinese on stagecoach to goldfields, author unknown between circa 1900 and circa 1920 [Public domain], via Wikimedia Commons, p10b Chinese employed by U.S. Army to work repairing ships in Australia c1944, courtesy of the State Library of Victoria [Public Domain], p12bl Lady Denman 1913-03-12 Canberra naming ceremony, courtesy of National Archives of Australia item 11399703, via Wikimedia Commons, p13tr Black leather lash with wooden handle, courtesy of National Museum of Australia [Public Domain], p14b 1914 International Lawn Tennis Challenge, by J. Parmley Paret [Public domain], via Wikimedia Commons, p13m Schoolchildren line up for free issue of soup and a slice of bread in the Depression, Belmore North Public School, Sydney, 2 August 1934, by Sam Hood (3550268287), courtesy of State Library of New South Wales collection [No restrictions], p13b primary school in the Beaconsfield district south-east of Melbourne in 1895, Spinning Tops and Gumdrops: A Portrait of Colonial Childhood by Edwin Barnard, p14mṛ Marn grook illustration 1857, by Gustav Mützel [Public domain], via Wikimedia Commons, p15tr Davis Cup Praha ČRo 2012-11-28 cropped 1, by Draceane [CC BY-SA 3.0 (https://creativeCommons.org/licenses/by-sa/3.0)], via Wikimedia Commons, p15bl The Sydney Gazette and New South Wales Advertiser (NSW : 1803 - 1842) Sat 6 Oct 1810, courtesy of National Museum of Australia [Public Domain], p16t Viewing west from southern bastion, by Peter L Johnson [CC BY-SA 3.0 (https:// creativeCommons.org/licenses/by-sa/3.0)], via Wikimedia Commons, p17bl Bombing of Darwin, courtesy of RAN Historical Collection [Public domain], via Wikimedia Commons, p18tr Holey dollar coinage NSW 1813 a128577 02 , courtesy of State Library of New South Wales [Public Domain], p21b Canvas town south melbourne victoria 1850s, courtesy of State Library of Victoria [Public domain], p22t The first Sydney post office, courtesy of State Library NSW, FL1231544 [Public Domain], p22b Aboriginal man carrying a message stick 1914, courtesy of State Library of South Australia [Public Domain], 23bl Overland Telegraph 1870, courtesy of State Library of Victoria [Public domain], p24t St Philips Church, by Pickering, Charles Percy (New South Wales. Government Printing Office), courtesy of State Library NSW, FL1231544 [Public Domain], p27 Yes for Aborigines, by Felix Farley [CC BY-SA 4.0 (https://creativeCommons.org/licenses/by-sa/4.0)], via Wikimedia Commons, p29t Emigration to Queensland - a broadsheet poster designed to attract migrants, 1899, courtesy of John Oxley Library, State Library of Queensland [Public Domain], p32br NSW Colonial Government - Ticket of Leave Passport, courtesy of Charles White [Public domain], via Wikimedia Commons.

NATIONAL LIBRARY OF AUSTRALIA
A catalogue record for this book is available from the National Library of Australia

CONTENTS

Fort Denison, Sydney

Oldest Continuous Culture on Earth

65,000 YEARS AGO

Australian Aboriginal people have the oldest continuous culture on Earth. They have been in Australia for at least 65,000 years, and the timeline is being pushed further back all the time as archaeologists make new discoveries. The very first human beings anywhere may have left Africa about 70,000 to 100,000 years ago, so the ancestors of the Australian Aboriginal people undertook one of the earliest mass migrations in history.

ICE AGE PEOPLE

During the last global Ice Age, which ended about 10,000 years ago, the Tasmanian Aboriginal people were probably the most southerly community on Earth. They lived through times of severe cold, ice and snow, developing clothing, habitation and hunting styles that enabled them to survive.

LOWER SEA LEVELS

Earth's sea levels were once lower than they are today. People travelled across dry land and shallow seas from the north as part of humanity's great wave of ancient migration around the globe.

HOW MANY PEOPLE?

The Aboriginal population of Australia before the first British settlers arrived in 1788 could have been between 300,000 and 1,000,000 people. The 2016 census reports that there are now about 798,000 Aboriginal Australians. They make up about 3.3% of Australia's population.

ANCIENT ART

Some of the oldest rock art sites in the whole world are located in Australia. The pictures and symbols were carved or painted on the rock's surface. The stencilled hands were made by blowing paint around a hand. The only known ancient, full-body stencil made in this way is in the Carnarvon National Park in Queensland.

FREEDOM RIDE

In 1965, a group of Sydney University students, including Charles Perkins, toured New South Wales raising awareness of the need to remove discrimination against Aboriginal people in country towns.

FUR CLOAKS

Aboriginal people living in the cooler parts of Australia made fur cloaks from animal skins. Drawings by colonists show the cloaks being worn with the fur on the inside for warmth.

SECOND WORLD WAR

The Tiwi people on Melville Island patrolled their region to look for any advance warnings of Japanese invasion during the Second World War. They captured the first Japanese prisoner of war when his aircraft crashed onto the island.

THE APOLOGY

In 2008, Prime Minister Kevin Rudd made a formal apology in Parliament to Australia's Indigenous people. The apology regretted the suffering caused for the Stolen Generations, and for past laws that discriminated against Indigenous people.

French, Dutch or British?

PARLEZ-VOUS FRANCAIS?

Australia might have become a French instead of a British colony if the First Fleet had arrived later than it did. On the very same day that Governor Phillip brought the ships of the First Fleet into Sydney Harbour in 1788, French captain La Perouse was sailing in the area, taking a look around to see what was going on. He was acting under instructions from King Louis XVI of France to explore the Pacific, including the new southern land found by James Cook eighteen years before. King Louis XVI and Queen Marie Antoinette were both executed during the French Revolution, which began in 1789.

SPANISH OR DUTCH?

During the great age of naval exploration in the 1500s, the countries of Europe had a treaty that divided the world into regions of ownership. Imaginary lines drawn across the globe gave all land to European powers. Although Australia was an unknown land at the time, parts of it technically belonged for a time to Spain and later to Holland through the Dutch East India Company. This division did not last forever. Britain had claimed the entire eastern half by 1770, and eventually claimed all of the western part of Australia too.

CAPTAIN COOK WASN'T A CAPTAIN

We all refer to Captain Cook as the man who explored the east coast of Australia in 1770, but he wasn't actually a captain at the time. His rank was lieutenant when he first sailed along Australia's east coast, and he was promoted to a higher rank on his return to England.

DUTCH EAST INDIA COMPANY

The Dutch East India Company, or VOC, was one of the largest and most powerful global businesses that has ever existed. Privately owned, yet acting with the approval of the Dutch government, the VOC colonised whole countries, sent out explorers to find new ones, and controlled a large part of world trade, particularly the immensely valuable spice trade. In the 1600s, ships of the VOC visited Australia in search of lands to conquer. After encountering the Aboriginal people, and finding they were prepared to fight aggressively to defend their land, the VOC ships sailed on. The Dutch could see no purpose in engaging in battle over a land that seemed to be no more than dry, worthless desert.

'UNFIT FOR HUMAN HABITATION'

In the late 1600s, before anyone in Europe knew that the continent of Australia existed, the British sent William Dampier on an expedition into the area. Part pirate and part government sponsored, Dampier found the northwest coast of Western Australia. After taking a brief look around, he declared the whole land 'unfit for human habitation'. This unfavourable report kept other explorers away for decades. In 1770, James Cook finally claimed the east coast for Britain.

Portrait of a senior merchant of the Dutch East India Shipping Company

First Fleet

HOW MANY PEOPLE CAME FIRST?

The first British people to live in Australia came in 1788 on eleven ships. The people on these sailing ships included about 780 male and female convicts, and about 550 other people who were marines, British naval officers and a few free settlers.

AS SMALL AS A MANLY FERRY

The First Fleet ships were small – no larger than a modern Manly ferry carrying commuters across Sydney harbour. With over 1,300 men, women and children, the fleet took eight months to reach its destination on the coast of New South Wales. As well as people, the ships also carried horses, cows, pigs, sheep, goats, chickens and rabbits.

WHO WERE THE MARINES?

The marines who guarded the convicts on the ships and in the colony after landing were not ordinary members of the Royal Navy. They were a special group of men who had been recruited just for this purpose. Not above committing crimes themselves, some marines were hung for stealing food soon after landing.

WHICH SHIP CAME FIRST?

Governor Phillip was on the HMS Supply when it sailed into Port Jackson on the evening of 25 January, 1788. He stayed on board overnight and in the morning was rowed to the shore. He landed at a spot near where Sydney's Circular Quay is today, raised the Union Jack, the flag of Great Britain, and announced that the colony and all the land belonged to Britain.

Governor Arthur Phillip

Those Convict Ancestors

CONVICTS OR SLAVES?

Being a convict in the early colonies was much like being a slave. Men, women and sometimes even children were given to free settlers as workers. In return for the convicts' labour, the government expected the settlers to provide their workers with food and somewhere to sleep. Male convicts worked on farms or helped to build houses, fences and anything else that was needed. Female convicts worked in households as cooks, servants and housekeepers.

TICKET OF LEAVE

The early colony in New South Wales did not have the funds, materials or workers to build prisons to house all the convicts. As a result, some convicts were allowed to go out into the community and start businesses or take up paying jobs. These men and women had a Ticket of Leave, which enabled them to live fairly normal lives, marry and even bring their families from Britain.

RIOT IN THE SUBURBS

The Castle Hill Rebellion of 1804 erupted just a short horse ride away from the centre of Sydney. Women living nearby fled to Sydney for safety as flames from burning buildings at Castle Hill lit the sky. The Governor in Sydney joined his troops on an overnight march and they reached Castle Hill the next day. The rioters were mostly Irish convicts, many of them political prisoners, whose aim was to overthrow the local authorities and then return to Ireland. They did not succeed, and the consequences for the rioters were very severe. Many died during the battle, and others were later executed.

Riot at Castle Hill

All the Way From China

WALK TO CHINA

The convicts who came to Australia after 1788 often had very little knowledge of world geography. Some of them hoped to escape to China, which they thought was just a few days walk away through the bush.

NEW GOLD MOUNTAIN

The discovery of gold in the 1850s enticed thousands of Chinese men to leave their villages in southern China to dig for gold in Australia. They nicknamed Australia the 'New Gold Mountain'. Not all of the Chinese miners became rich from digging for gold. Some opened the very first Chinese restaurants in Australia, feeding other diggers on the goldfields.

CHINESE ON CONVOYS

The Second World War in the Pacific region threatened Australia with invasion and destruction of its whole way of life. Soldiers sent north to fight in the islands and Papua New Guinea travelled in groups of ships called convoys. These ships all needed kitchens, cleaning and other basic services to keep the men fit and ready for battle. Australia's population was so small in the 1940s that there were not enough local soldiers to fill all these roles. The government decided to recruit Chinese sailors to provide the services needed.

Chinese man repairing a ship in Australia, 1940s

Superstitions From the Old Country

YOWIES, YETIS AND HAIRY MONSTERS

All across the world, people tell stories of hairy, human-like creatures that roam wild, deserted places. Australia has its own yowie stories, and they range from reports of people seeing strange, ape-sized creatures in the bush, to actual close encounters. When the sighting turns out to be a person wearing a badly-fitting ape costume, it is very disappointing for those who want to believe that yowies really do exist.

DAISY WHEELS

The Richmond Courthouse in Tasmania has examples of daisy wheel carvings in some of its woodwork. These are protective symbols that come from the beliefs of folk religions, once common throughout Britain. The complex circles in a daisy wheel were supposed to confuse any evil influences and keep people nearby safe.

CORN DOLLIES

Corn dollies are shapes or little figures made out of dried corn or wheat stalks. In Europe they were a feature of folk religions that centred on the importance of the harvest. The Europeans who came to the Australian colonies to start a new life brought with them the tradition of making corn dollies. Craft shops across Australia often sell little corn dollies made by the locals. The Shire of Koorda in Western Australia's wheat growing region calls itself Corn Dolly Country.

CATS AND SHOES

When early settlers came to Australia from 1788 onward, they brought their superstitions with them. In some parts of England, builders would place a dead cat inside the walls of a new house as a good luck charm, and this tradition ended up in Australia too. People in Australia who are renovating their colonial houses sometimes find the skeleton of a cat in the walls, put there to keep the inhabitants safe from evil influences. Shoes were another good luck charm that sometimes ended up inside house walls.

Pick a Name

WHAT'S THAT PLACE CALLED?

The first settlers in 1788 named their collection of tents and rough timber huts Sydney Town, but they were keen to find out the Aboriginal names for places too. Since the Eora people and the British did not understand each other's language, a lot of pointing at places inevitably ended up with the wrong word being used as a local name for a place or feature of the land. For example, the name for Coogee Beach in Sydney may refer to a place that has a bad smell, due to the decaying seaweed.

WAS LADY DENMAN RIGHT OR WRONG?

What is the correct pronunciation of Canberra, the name of Australia's capital city? Is it two syllables or three? The name chosen for the capital city was kept a secret by the government until Lady Denman, wife of the Governor, announced it at a ceremony held in 1913. The name was written on a card and placed inside a little golden box. In front of the assembled crowd, she opened the box and told them the name, pronouncing it as Can'bra with two syllables. That's the reason we now all use her pronunciation, instead of using three syllables to say the name of Australia's capital city.

Children

YOUNGEST CONVICT

The youngest convict sentenced to transportation and ending up in New South Wales was John Hudson. He was tried for theft when he was only nine years old. His parents were dead and he had worked as a chimneysweep to support himself. Young John lived a harsh life, at one time receiving a punishment of fifty lashes for not keeping to the rules.

CURRENCY CHILDREN

In the 1800s, children of convicts in the new colony were known by the term 'currency', while the children of the free settlers were called 'sterling'. The currency children grew up in surroundings that were very different from those they would have experienced back in Britain. They were healthier, taller and developed a local accent. Visitors to the colony also noted that these currency children were less likely to consider themselves inferior to the upper classes.

CHILDREN DURING THE GREAT DEPRESSION

In the 1930s, Australians suffered through an economic depression. Around a third of all wage earners became unemployed. At the time, men were usually the main income earner for their families and their mass unemployment meant that children were often hungry and poorly clothed. Many families were evicted when they could not pay their rents, and children and their parents then had to find shelter wherever they could. Their new dwellings included tents, caves and shacks made from discarded pieces of timber, hessian and iron sheeting.

Primary school, Beaconsfield, Melbourne, 1895

GOING TO SCHOOL

Convicts who were children were supposed to work, not go to school. The children of free settlers had a private tutor or attended one of the private or church schools. By the end of the 1800s, compulsory education for all children usually lasted until they were fourteen years old. Many children left school to work at that age, and finishing high school was not a priority for them. Attending university was a privilege for only a small number of young people.

Aussies Love Their Sport

Panathenaic Stadium, Athens.
Site of the first Olympic Games

WE ONLY HAD ONE OLYMPIAN

The world's first Modern Olympic Games held in Athens in 1896 had only one competitor from colonial Australia. Edwin Flack competed in a number of events and won two medals.

ABORIGINAL CRICKET TEAM

The first Australian cricket team to visit England was made up of thirteen Aboriginal team members. They made headlines wherever they played on their 1868 tour, winning fourteen out of forty-seven games.

SPORT ON TV

The Olympic Games held in Melbourne in 1956 were the first Olympics ever broadcast on Australian television. People all around Australia could watch the competitions in their own homes as long as they owned a television. TVs were very expensive, and those who could not afford to buy one crowded around shop windows where a television was turned on to show the Olympic Games to potential customers.

Television set, 1950s

MARNGROOK

Marngrook is an Indigenous game that uses a ball made of possum skin. Jumping high to catch the ball is a feature of Marngrook. This traditional football-style game comes from Victoria and may have influenced the development of Australian Rules Football.

FIRST TENNIS TOURNAMENTS

From the late 1800s, the Melbourne Cricket Club became a major organiser of lawn tennis championships in Australia. In the following years, tennis gained in popularity as a pastime, although not everyone could afford access to tennis courts and equipment. Up until 1914, both Australia and New Zealand competed in the Davis Cup together as a joint Australasian team.

1914 Davis Cup finals match between Australasia and the United States

Davis Cup Trophy

HORSE RACING

The first public horse race was held in Sydney Town in 1810 at Hyde Park, which at that time had been cleared of trees. Governor Macquarie tried to avoid any public disorder at this exciting event by issuing the following order to all the residents:

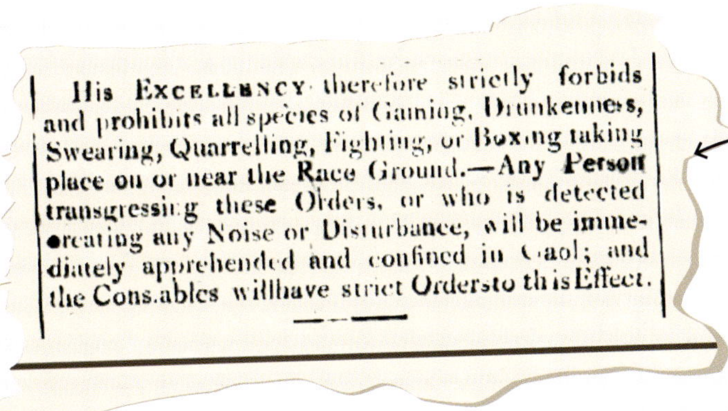

His EXCELLENCY therefore strictly forbids and prohibits all species of Gaming, Drunkenness, Swearing, Quarrelling, Fighting, or Boxing taking place on or near the Race Ground.—Any Person transgressing these Orders, or who is detected creating any Noise or Disturbance, will be immediately apprehended and confined in Gaol; and the Constables willhave strict Ordersto thisEffect.

Sydney Gazette, 6 October, 1810

"His Excellency therefore strictly forbids and prohibits all species of Gaming, Drunkenness, Swearing, Quarrelling, Fighting, or Boxing taking place on or near the Race Ground. Any Person transgressing these Orders, or who is detected creating any Noise or Disturbance, will be immediately apprehended and confined in Gaol."

Defending Australia

PINCHGUT

In Sydney's harbour there is a tiny island that used to be called Pinchgut. Once a place for hangings and exile for convicts, Pinchgut was later the site of important structures for the colony's defence. Renamed Fort Denison in the 1850s, the island housed cannons and military quarters. Its purpose was to provide protection from enemy ships that might decide to sail into the harbour and attack Sydney.

SLOUCH HAT

The Australian Army's distinctive Slouch Hat has a long history. Traditionally worn with the side pinned up, the broad-brimmed hat is made from rabbit fur felt or wool felt. The band around the crown is called a puggaree. The hat is turned up on one side so that the brim does not get in the way of the rifle during drill movements. Although soldiers wore various styles before Federation, by 1903 all Australian soldiers wore a standard shape of Slouch Hat. The name is a reference to the downward sloping brim.

RISING SUN BADGE

The badge in the shape of a rising sun is worn on the upturned side of the Slouch Hat. The exact shape of the badge has changed a number of times since soldiers first began wearing it in the early 1900s. On the first design, the rays of the sun were represented by swords and bayonets.

JERVIS BAY

Jervis Bay on the southeast coast of Australia has a close connection with Canberra and the ACT (Australian Capital Territory). Located about 250 kilometres from Canberra, Jervis Bay was set aside by the founders of Federation as Australia's national naval port. It was to be the centre of the Commonwealth's naval defence operations.

DARWIN BOMBED

The explosion of MV Neptuna, Darwin 1942

In 1942, during the Second World War, Japanese aircraft bombed Darwin in a raid that shocked all Australians. There were bombing raids on other towns as well, although these are not written about as often. Up until the end of 1943, there were over 200 raids undertaken by the Japanese air force. The towns of Broome, Derby, Katherine, Port Hedland, Townsville and Wyndham were all bombed during this time.

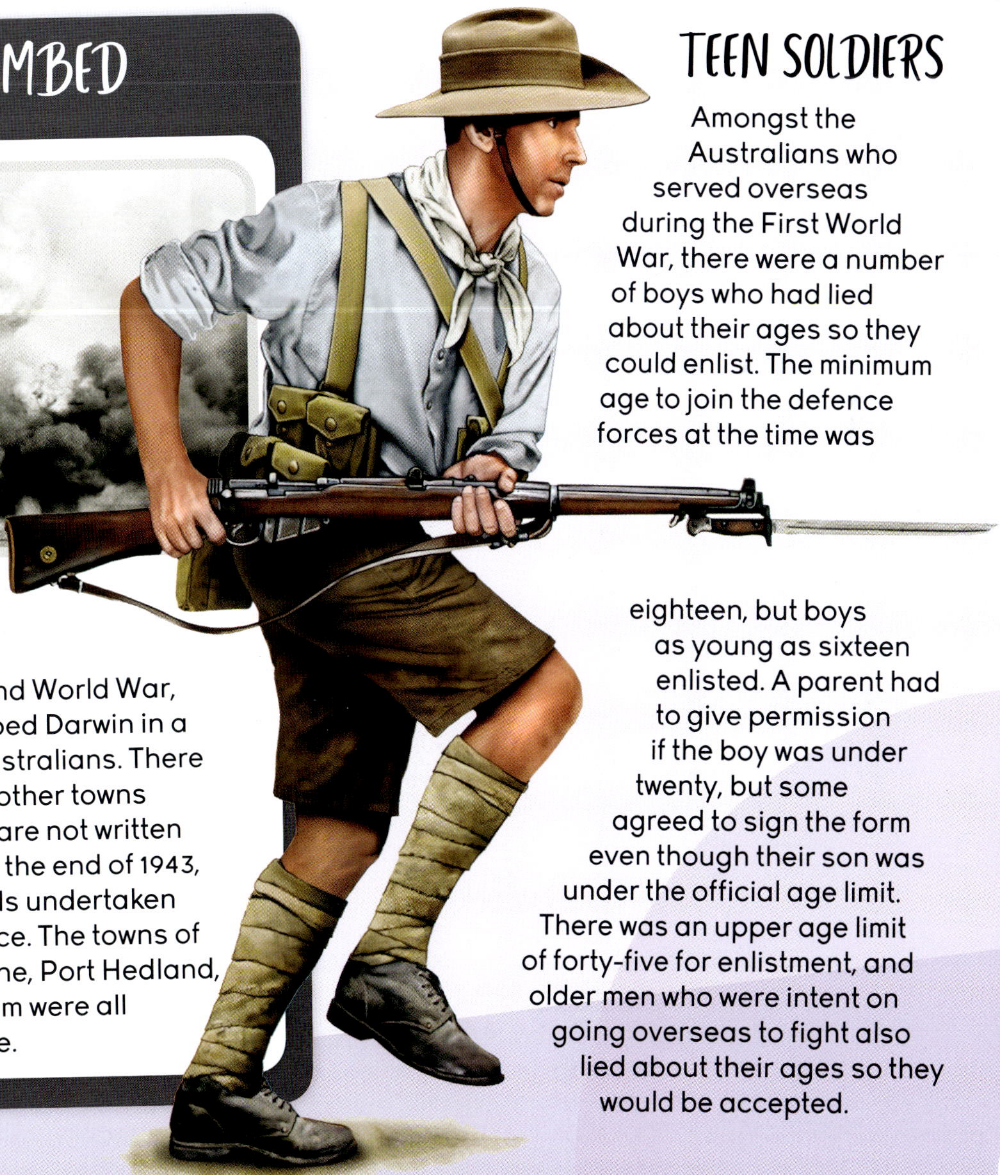

TEEN SOLDIERS

Amongst the Australians who served overseas during the First World War, there were a number of boys who had lied about their ages so they could enlist. The minimum age to join the defence forces at the time was eighteen, but boys as young as sixteen enlisted. A parent had to give permission if the boy was under twenty, but some agreed to sign the form even though their son was under the official age limit. There was an upper age limit of forty-five for enlistment, and older men who were intent on going overseas to fight also lied about their ages so they would be accepted.

Shopping

AUSTRALIA'S FIRST MONEY WAS FULL OF HOLES

There were not enough coins to go around back in 1810, so Governor Macquarie had to do something about it. He sent word back to Britain that his little colony needed coins. When the coins arrived, Macquarie doubled their number by arranging to have a small piece cut out of each. The outer ring became known as a holey dollar, and the inner piece was called a dump. Examples of each are now highly prized by collectors of old coins.

YO HO HO AND A BOTTLE OF RUM

It wasn't only pirates who loved their rum. Residents of Sydney Town in the early 1800s collected it as well. Rum became the money of the time, and people traded it to pay wages and buy food. The first hospital in Sydney was called the Rum Hospital because its builders received rum instead of money for their wages.

GROCERY DELIVERIES BY CAMELS

Right up until the early 1900s, grocery deliveries to outback areas across Australia's dry, desert regions came by camel. Afghan camel drivers provided a vital service to remote regions which had no other way of receiving regular deliveries of things they needed. The camels were much better suited to the desert conditions than horses, and their Afghan handlers had a legendary status in the outback regions where they used to work. The train that runs between Adelaide and Darwin is called The Ghan in memory of the Afghan cameleers.

NO SHOPS ON SUNDAYS

Going to shops on Sundays is only a recent way for Australians to spend their weekends. Up until the mid 1900s, most shops were not allowed to open on Sundays. Shops closed at 12 noon on Saturdays as well, so if you ran out of milk there was frequently nowhere to buy any until the shops reopened on Monday morning.

Where Did You Get That Dress?

FASHION

Dress style, early 1800s

Clothes in the early 1800s were expensive and difficult to obtain. Much of the cotton for dresses and shirts came from India, as did the embroidered shawls that were a favourite with women who could afford to buy them. One of these shawls made a perfect gift and women proudly wore them as they walked around the streets of early Sydney and Hobart Town.

Although we tend to think of women's clothing during the colonial era as being very heavy and multi-layered, this was only the case in later years. In the early 1800s, the fashionable style was a simple dress made of a type of light cotton called muslin. This Empire Style was short enough to show the ankles and allowed bare arms and shoulders. The obvious practicality of the Empire Style for the hot Australian summers was ignored by the mid 1800s, as the tightly corsetted clothing of the Victorian era became the fashion.

FOOD SACKS AND LICE

The convict women had to wear the prison clothing they were given. On the First Fleet, the problem with lice became so bad that on one of the ships all of the convict women's clothes had to be destroyed. The women were given new dresses made out of spare food sacks.

What's For Dinner?

SALTED MEAT AND PEAS

The first settlers lived mainly on dried foods that they had brought with them. It was months before they could grow crops, and they were wary of trying anything that grew locally. When the dried meat and peas ran out, they all nearly starved, despite the fact that there was an abundance of bush food all around them.

CURRY

In the 1800s, when the early colonists were trying to survive at Sydney Cove, many of them longed for a good curry to eat. Today, most of us imagine that curries are a recent favourite, brought to Australia by people migrating recently from India. Not so! The colony at Sydney Town had close connections with India. Local settlers waited impatiently for the arrival of sailing ships bringing cotton, rice and curry powder for sale. Some of the naval men in the colony had spent time in India, and grew to like the food there. When they came to Sydney, they brought their newly acquired taste for curry with them.

ICE FROM AMERICA

In the mid 1800s, people living in Sydney and Melbourne did not have refrigerators to keep food and drinks cool. When sailing ships arrived carrying blocks of ice cut out of frozen lakes in Boston, America, people flocked to buy a piece. The ice was packed in straw and sawdust, but a lot of it still melted on the long journey to Australia. A series of hot Sydney summers, with temperatures over 40°C, resulted in the imported ice becoming a popular but expensive novelty.

Home Sweet Home

BARK AND SLAB HUTS

The bark and slab huts built by early settlers were only ever meant to be temporary. Every settler hoped to one day build a permanent home for their family and replace the bark or slab hut that was quick to build and gave them basic shelter. Remarkably, bark and slab huts survived for an exceptionally long time, despite the effects of rough weather and termites.

1850s gold digger's hut of canvas and bark

Old bush hut

TENT CITIES

British settlement in Australia began as a town of tents in Sydney, and settlers throughout Australia all lived at first in tents. In 1829, Governor Stirling administered Perth from a tent, and his young wife looked after their two children there as well. In Melbourne, the Gold Rush of the 1850s resulted in a new tent city being established as the only way to house the large numbers of people who were flocking there as a stopover on their way to the goldfields.

1850s canvas town south Melbourne, Victoria

PREFABRICATED BUILDINGS

Buildings that are made up in pieces, then sent to locations to be assembled on site, are not a new idea. There was a prefabricated wooden house amongst the items sent on the First Fleet. This was to be the official residence for Governor Phillip, ensuring that his social standing and authority were not diminished by having to give orders from a tent for more than a few days after stepping ashore in 1788.

AUSTRALIAN BUNGALOW

The colonial houses that Australians now preserve and treasure were designed according to a layout that was popular in India. The wide verandas and rooms that have access to the garden were all developed for the hot, humid climates of southern India. Many of the military officials and merchants who came to colonial Australia had lived in these types of houses in India and they found them more suited to the local weather than the traditional English style of house, with its small, enclosed rooms and lack of outdoor living areas.

Keeping in Touch

DANGERS OF MAIL DELIVERY

In the colonial era, delivering mail outside the main towns could be a dangerous undertaking. Bushrangers attacked the mail carriers, hoping to find valuables amongst the letters and parcels. There was often the problem of muddy tracks and floods to overcome, as well as keeping the horses fit and healthy on the journey.

Sydney's first post office, opened 1810

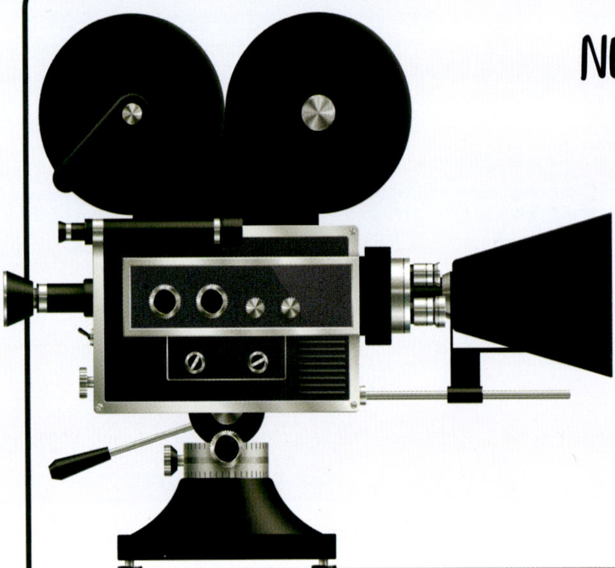

NEWSREELS AT THE MOVIES

Before television brought news programs into people's homes, the only way for the public to see film of news events was to watch them at the movies. Before the main movie there was usually a news show, with current events from Australia and the world. Called newsreels, these films were in black and white, with background music and sometimes sensational headlines. Some theatres specialised in showing news all day, and people would drop in to see the latest events and then leave as the newsreel repeated itself.

MESSAGE STICKS

Message sticks inscribed with symbols are an Australian Aboriginal invention used to exchange information over long distances. Carried by the message bearer, the symbols and markings on the sticks were a written code that neighbouring nations could read. The message content could be about trade or plans for a meeting.

NO PHONES, INTERNET, RADIO OR TV

Without a telephone or the internet, how would you contact people living on the other side of Australia, or even just in the next town? The first telegraph service began in Australia in 1854. Before then, the only way to communicate over long distances was to send a letter, which travelled initially in a slow sailing ship or was carried by a horse rider.

A	• —	N	— •	1	• — — — —	?	• • — — • •
B	— • • •	O	— — —	2	• • — — —	!	— • — • — —
C	— • — •	P	• — — •	3	• • • — —	,	— — • • — —
D	— • •	Q	— — • —	4	• • • • —	.	— • — • — •
E	•	R	• — •	5	• • • • •		
F	• • — •	S	• • •	6	— • • • •		
G	— — •	T	—	7	— — • • •		
H	• • • •	U	• • —	8	— — — • •		
I	• •	V	• • • —	9	— — — — •		
J	• — — —	W	• — —	0	— — — — —		
K	— • —	X	— • • —				
L	• — • •	Y	— • — —				
M	— —	Z	— — • •				

The telegraph service used wires and Morse Code to send messages. People who could understand Morse Code sent the message using a special machine and then the message had to be decoded at the other end. The operator produced a handwritten telegram and then had it delivered to the house or business of the person it was addressed to. Telegrams were costly to send, so they were only used for important messages. The knock at the door of the 'telegram boy' was often a stressful occasion, as people knew it meant they were about to receive either very good or very bad news.

When it happened in Australia

1854	local telegraph service
1872	overseas telegraph service
1880s	local telephone services
1920s	first radio broadcasts to the general public
1956	black and white TV
1975	colour TV
1980s	first local mobile phones

Building the Overland Telegraph Line, 1870

Mobile phone, 1980

Religion

AUSTRALIA'S FIRST AND ONLY SAINT

Saint Mary MacKillop is Australia's first Saint of the Roman Catholic Church. In 1866, in South Australia, she helped to found the religious order called the Sisters of Saint Joseph of the Sacred Heart. In true Australian style, she would oppose church authorities if she believed what they were doing was not right, putting the welfare of the people before herself. She took a stand at a time in history when women rarely defied the senior authority in churches or any other powerful organisations in society.

CATHOLICS AND PROTESTANTS

The oldest Anglican church in Australia, Saint Philip's Church, Sydney

The Roman Catholic Church and the Church of England (now the Anglican Church) operated in opposition to each other during the early days of settlement. The history of war and distrust between the two religions in Britain affected the way the settlers behaved towards each other in Australia as well. Catholic priests were not welcome in the colony until Fathers Therry and Conolly arrived in 1820, thirty-two years after Sydney was founded.

CHURCH ATTENDANCE COMPULSORY

Convicts in the early settlement at Sydney Cove had to attend church every Sunday. In 1791, Governor Phillip ordered that convicts who did not turn up at church on Sundays would have their food rations reduced.

MOSQUES IN THE DESERT

The Afghan camel drivers who first came to Australia in the 1800s constructed small mosques throughout the desert regions where they worked. In 1888, Adelaide became the first large city in Australia to have its own mosque.

Afghan mosque, Queensland

Getting to Know the Neighbours

MACASSANS

The Australian Aboriginal people living along the northern coast of the continent formed trading ties with people from islands that are now part of Indonesia. Once called Macassans, the people who came across the sea to trade made temporary camps in Australia. The tamarind trees that still grow in the region are mostly descendants of trees planted there by Macassans, often hundreds of years ago, long before the British settlers arrived. The trading history of the Yolngu Aboriginal people is evident in the presence of Macassan words in the Yolngu language.

NEW ZEALAND THE 7TH STATE?

When the British first claimed the east coast of Australia, they also claimed New Zealand. In 1788, when Arthur Phillip arrived at Port Jackson with the First Fleet, his authority as Governor extended all the way to New Zealand.

PAPUA NEW GUINEA

Spain, Portugal, Germany and Britain were all interested in controlling the resources of Papua New Guinea. In the late 1800s, Germany claimed the northern region, while Britain claimed the southern section. After the First World War ended in 1918, the Commonwealth of Australia gained full control over all of Papua New Guinea. PNG became a fully independent nation in 1975.

Kings and Queens

GOD SAVE THE QUEEN

Before 1984, when Advance Australia Fair became the national anthem, people used to sing God Save the Queen instead. In movie theatres, before the show started, everyone stood and sang God Save the Queen. At the Melbourne Olympic Games in 1956, Australia's medal winners stood proudly on the podium while God Save the Queen rang out around them.

PRINCES IN DANGER

Two British princes have been attacked by protesters while visiting Australia. In 1994, an assailant shot at Prince Charles with a starting pistol. In 1868, Prince Albert, son of Queen Victoria, was shot and wounded by a protester.

WEDDING GIFTS

Governments in Australia traditionally send wedding gifts when a member of the Royal Family gets married. In 1947, when Princess Elizabeth was married, the Queensland Government sent the unusual gift of 500 tins of pineapple. These were later distributed to charities.

PRINCESS MARY

Australia now has a close connection with the monarchy of another country besides Great Britain. In 2004, Mary Donaldson from Tasmania married Crown Prince Frederik of Denmark. When the Prince becomes King, his Australian-born wife will become Queen Mary, although her official title will be Mary, Queen Consort of Denmark.

Governing Ourselves

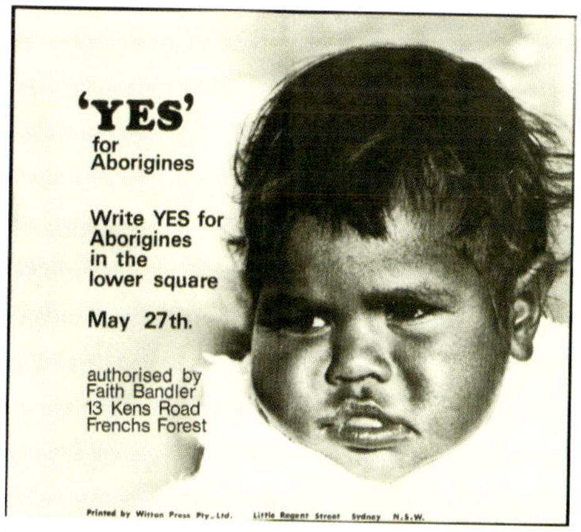

WOMEN NOT ALLOWED TO VOTE

Allowing women to vote in elections is a fairly recent right around the world. In Australia, the first state to allow women to vote was South Australia in 1894. The last state was Victoria in 1908. In comparison to other western nations, Australia was very progressive. In the USA, women could not vote until 1920, and in Britain they gained a limited right to vote in 1918.

ABORIGINAL CITIZENSHIP

Up until 1967, Australian Aboriginal people were not considered to be citizens of Australia. This shameful situation changed after a referendum was held. The result of the vote was that 90% of Australians agreed that Aboriginal Australians must have full rights as citizens.

BRITISH SUBJECTS

Even though Australia became an independent nation in 1901, many Australians were still proud of their British heritage. In fact, before 1949, there was no such thing as an Australian citizen, and Australians were legally British subjects.

FORGOTTEN RELIC OF THE FEDERATION CEREMONY, 1901

The Australian Federation ceremony took place in 1901 underneath an ornate pavilion erected in Centennial Park in Sydney. Sixty thousand people attended, and every dignitary in Australia was there. Although the pavilion looked very grand, it was made mostly of plaster, so it could not be left out in the weather permanently. All the plaster decorations were later removed, and what was left of the pavilion ended up in a suburban park at Cabarita in Sydney. The huge slab of granite on which the pavilion originally stood could not be moved and remains in Centennial Park, where it now forms the basis of a commemorative building.

Aussies Come From Everywhere

HOW MANY PEOPLE?

Of the 25 million adults and children in Australia, about 67% of them were born in Australia and 33% were born overseas. A very large percentage of Australian-born people have at least one parent who was born overseas.

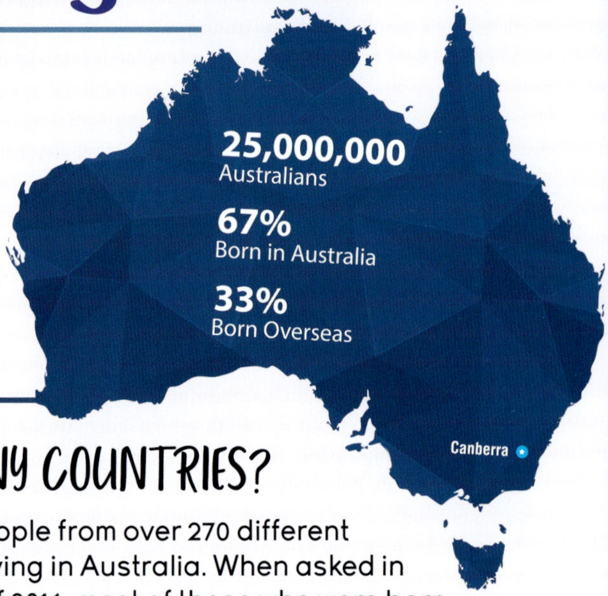

WHO CAME FIRST?

The Australian Aboriginal peoples came first. With a local heritage dating back 65,000 years, no other group can match them for length of time living on the Australian continent.

HOW MANY COUNTRIES?

There are people from over 270 different ancestries living in Australia. When asked in the census of 2016, most of those who were born overseas reported that they had come from England, New Zealand, China, India and the Philippines. Many of these people have lived in Australia for years, but recent migration sources are revealing a new pattern. The top sources of migration to Australia now also include Pakistan, Vietnam and South Africa.

MALE AND FEMALE

There is a slightly higher number of female than male people in Australia.

Male	49.3%
Female	50.7%

LEAVING THE OLD DART

Migrants from England and Ireland in the 18th and 19th centuries sometimes referred to their homeland as The Old Dart. The origin of this slang term may be a reference to the English port area called Dartmouth. Thousands of migrants have arrived in Australia from Britain, many more than from any other country. Migration posters designed to attract British people to Australia emphasised the warm climate and healthy surroundings they would find if they emigrated.

Emigration to Queensland.

Nominated Passengers. Permanent residents in Queensland wishing to obtain passages for their friends or relatives in the United Kingdom or the Continent of Europe nay do so under the provisions of the Immigration Act, by making payments to the Immigration Agent in Brisbane, r the Assistant Immigration Agents, Maryborough, Bundaberg, Rockhampton, Mackay or Townsville, or to the Clerks f Petty Sessions at any other town in the Colony upon the following scale :—

MALES between one and twelve years, £2 ; between twelve and forty, £4 ; over forty and under fifty-five, £8.
FEMALES between one and twelve, £1 ; between twelve and forty, £2 ; over forty and under fifty-five, £8.
MALES or FEMALES—fifty-five and upwards, the full passage money, £13 13s.

Assisted Passengers. The Agent-General for Queensland (whose address is Westminster Chambers, No. 1 Victoria Street, London, S.W.), will entertain applicaons for some assistance towards the total cost of passage from small capitalist Farmers, Market Gardeners, Dairymen nd Orchardists—especially in the case of those having families. Full particulars as to the occupations of the head nd members of the family, their available Capital and intentions as to pursuit on landing, etc., should be forwarded ith the application and each case will be condered on its merits. Whatever money conibutions it may be decided to grant towards e cost of passage may apply to the case of ersons wishing to proceed to the colony either s second-class or as steerage passengers.

Full-Paying Passengers.

ny person whose application for an assisted assage cannot be entertained may, as heretore, avail himself of the third-class passenger ate namely, £13 13s. (including "ship kit") ranted by the British India Company's direct ne of Steamers from London to Queensland.

Free Passengers. Female Domestic ervants and Farm Labourers will be granted ree Passages to Queensland upon the aproval of the Agent-General for Queensland in ondon (whose address is Westminster Chamers, No. 1 Victoria Street, London, S.W.), nd forms of application setting forth the terms nd conditions upon which such passages will e granted may be obtained by communication ith the office of the Agent-General, who must e thoroughly satisfied with the character and *bona fides* of each applicant. The only outlay to be incurred by the migrant will be the cost of transit from his place of residence to the port of embarkation, and also the charge for ship kit," viz., £1.

IMMIGRATION OFFICE AND DEPOT, BRISBANE.

Reception in the Colony. All Emigrants, as enumerated above, will be accommodated, Free of all Expense, at the Immigration Depot at the port of arrival r 14 days, or such period as may enable them to complete their arrangements, and they will further be entitled to ceive a Free Pass to any part of the Colony where a railway line exists.

Queensland as a Home. The Climate is healthy and entirely free from rigorous extremes. The Soil in many parts is Rich and Productive and equal to anything be found in the world. A Splendid System of National Education prevails throughout the Colony which is solutely free to all classes. Freehold Farms of from 160 acres to 640 acres, according to quality of soil and distance om market, can be bought at the rate of 2s. 6d. per Acre, the purchase money being payable in yearly instalments of l. per acre, and extending over a period of Ten Years.

WAGES.—Farm Servants command from £35 to £50 per annum. Married Couples command up to £80 per nnum. Female Domestic Servants (including Cooks, Housemaids, General Servants and Dairymaids), from 8s. to per week. (In all above cases "Board and Lodging" is found.)

LEAVING AUSTRALIA

Although most of Australia's migration history is about people who chose Australia as their new home, there was one group that reversed this trend. In 1893, a group of people left Australia for Paraguay in South America to create what they thought would be their ideal colony. They named their settlement New Australia and some of their descendants are still living there.

LITTLE GREECE

Melbourne's Lonsdale Street Greek Precinct is a cultural hub for thousands of Greek migrant families in the city. Melbourne has long proudly announced to the world that it has the largest population of people with Greek heritage anywhere outside Greece itself.

Just a Little While Ago...

QUICK, TAKE A SELFIE!

Selfies are photos we take of ourselves on our mobile phones or tablets. Selfies of celebrities and famous people all around the world fill social media to bursting point! We're all obsessed with selfies, but did you know that the term was born in Australia? Oxford Dictionaries made 'selfie' their word of the year in 2013, and gave it an Australian origin.

PURPLE WEATHER

In 2013, the Australian Bureau of Meteorology had to add a new colour to its weather charts. Previously topped at 50°C, the Bureau's colour chart now has purple and pink added to represent any area on the map of Australia with a temperature range up to 54°C.

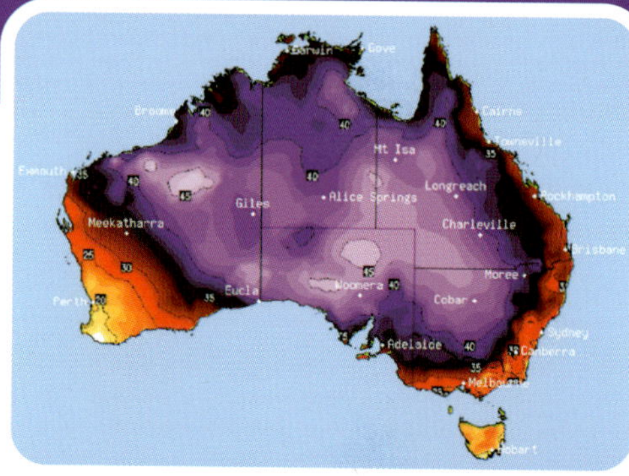

Glossary

archaeologist person who studies the remains of human history

bayonet dagger attached to a rifle

chimneysweep person who cleans the soot out of the inside of chimneys

commuter person who travels the same route often

corset tight underwear garment worn by women

folk religion religious beliefs that are not part of mainstream religions

hessian rough fabric

pastime hobby or recreational activity

quarters areas for living in

rum alcoholic drink

superstition belief in supernatural forces

tradition custom passed from ancestors to the present generation

Index

D. 17.

TICKET OF LEAVE PASSPORT.

No. 46/84

The Bearer John Rosser holding a Convict by the Ship Mel... Ticket of Leave No. 37/1056 for the District of Yass which is deposited in the Police Office at do which is deposited in the Police Office at and whose personal Description and Signature are on the other side, has obtained the permission of His Excellency the Governor to reside at Kyamba Creek Murrumbidgee in the Service of Messrs W Walker & Co.

for Twelve months, for the date hereof, conforming himself in every respect, according to the regulations laid down for the guidance of Convicts of his class.

Given at the Office of the Principal Superintendent of Convicts, Sydney, this thirteenth Day of February One Thousand Eight Hundred and forty six

Registered Thomas Ryan } Chief Clerk.